From the
HEART
of a
HORSEWOMAN

HORSE — A Bridge Between Spirit and Matter

Mystic Musing on the Horse/Human Relationship

LYNNEA PAXTON-HONN

Cover Art and *Heart Rider* by Valarie S. Roddy

Copyright 2020 Lynnea Honn

Published by Little Publishing Co.

Dedicated to all of my students who have challenged me to be the horsewoman that I am, to all of my mentors who guided me toward the skills for teaching my students, and to all of the horses that shared the journey with us.

Contents

...the power of Horse's Medicine was in the proper use of gifts, talents and abilities. Horse taught Two Leggeds to balance the tangible and intangible worlds. Like horse, Two leggeds were being taught to be of the Earth and to be at one with the wind. When the two worlds came together, balance was attained, allowing humans to see the beauty of spirit living and working through their physical form. Horse taught how to use will, endurance, authority and talents in a proper manner without abuse or misuse.

The 13 Original Clan Mothers, "Walks Tall Woman," Jamie Sams

Introduction

Was I born with the passion for horses? I don't know. I was born with a passion for life and horses are the epitome of life-energy, rhythm, beauty, symmetry, mystery, primordial connection to earth and heaven. I have spent much of my life wrapped in the pursuit of understanding the unifying essence that is created in the Horse/Human relationship. What I have learned is that there are no words to describe that instant of unity when bodies and minds meld into one intent, one dance, one expression.

When I was growing up, I spent my summers on the beach in a Southern California bay along the coast of the Pacific Ocean. Swimming out just past the breakers I would allow my body to float on the surface of the undulating sea, letting go and allowing the rhythmic surge of the water to hold and carry me. Just as I was lifted by the gentle heave of the ocean, in that place where tension and release are held together in mutual and balanced suspension, there is that moment when horse and rider release to the other, allowing form and movement to hold and carry them in one intent. In the presence of Horse I feel as though I am at the breast of the Mother; I hear her heartbeat, I taste her breath, I know her power, and I am accepted into that moment, that sense of just being. I am a piece of her and at peace with myself. It has been that way since the beginning, the first encounter.

I credit my fourth year of life as the year I was inducted into the Tribe of Horse by a gentle Palm Springs gelding who took the time and interest to introduce himself, and the world of horses, to me.

What does the path through this book look like? It is my search for the depth of the Horse/Human relationship through pondering, poetry, and study of the multifaceted interactions that bring such wonderful satisfaction to the mind, body, and soul. I explore practical and spiritual aspects of this amazing interspecies entanglement. It is my point of view that Horse is a bridge between matter and spirit if we are open to that journey. It is my intention to share what that paradigm means to me.

This is a spiritual compilation of writings about the horse, in human relationship, as the bridge between matter and spirit. Even though I have known this all along, I have been hesitant to share my mystic musings with an audience. This book cannot be completed without that acknowledgement.

In these writings I will use words describing the spirit bridge, the reach for experiential oneness. These words include God, Holy Spirit, and Oneness. These are not religious based words but words to take us to a place that contains wholeness, the completeness of the Horse/Human experience. Then again, the words of spirit are not limited to this relationship. As we explore, we discover life is all about relationship. This is just a spanning of the one passion for unity to a passion for unity in all of life. The very word "unity" holds its opposite, disunited or separate. In our quest for the perfect ride we are seeking unity on the level of wholeness or 'holiness.' This amazing, beautiful connection we have with horses is but a schooling place for the bigger connection that we have with all Life. This connection is in relationship, knowing that we are part of a whole ecosystem held in balance within our living home, The Earth, The Solar System, The Milky Way, The Universe.

A brief definition of these words:

God — All That Is, Oneness, The Source

Holy Spirit — the energy and essence of whole relationship

Soul — the essence of individual being that can relate with intuitive knowingness as a spark of the divine

Divine — life as sacred in its wholeness and its individuality — we are all divine sparks of Creation

Mystic — a mystic is one who places the experience of the spiritual above doctrine and dogma.

Gender — I chose to move between using "he" and "she" in this narrative. We each have our own favorite horses that come to mind as we read. This gives flexible opportunity to move between the genders — stallion, gelding, mare, colt, or filly.

Horse — "Horse" capitalized refers to the Archetype of Horse

2

If you have picked up this book you may already resonate with the awareness of Horse as the bridge to Spirit. You have an intuitive sense that waits at the edge of knowing. In the pursuit of horsemanship, we are searching for that ultimate space where horse and rider become one. One with each other in movement and intent. A combined consciousness that connects to each other and to a greater unity.

Part One
Personal Reflections on the Horse/Human Relationship

On the Nature of Horse

The nature of Horse is Spirit. Horse is first the embodiment of spirit in earth energy. Spirit is illuminated in horse by every symmetrical, rhythmic movement: the side-to-side swish of tail, the sound of chewing pasture grass, the flash of hooves as they kiss the ground.

The nature of Horse is Heart. It is the magnetic principal of heart, the synchronization and pull that draws us to Horse mystery, that silent beat that creates a primordial pounding in the Human pulse. Horse heart expands Human heart, frees it to blend with another.

The nature of Horse is Relationship. In relationship to each other and to the ecosystem of existence, Horse has lived thousands of years in successful interaction with all the nations of environment: animal, mineral, and plant. Horse brings Human into relationship with the kingdoms of nature.

The nature of Horse is Sensual. Horse lives the embodiment of senses: sight, sound, smell, touch, taste, far beyond the human sense realm. Horse offers Human an experience of expanded awareness.

Spirit

In his book, _Meditation for Two: Searching for and Finding Communion with Horses,_ Dominque Barbier writes, _"When man communicates with the horse it is on so many levels, but the most important is the spiritual. Who is closer to God than the horse?"_

Spirit — is it not spirit, and freedom in spirit manifested in Horse, that first brought us front and center into the world of horses? Spirit is such an elusive concept. It has many descriptions and definitions, all of which are metaphysical and unsubstantial, subtle in form. Spirit is unseen yet permeates all existence. How do we recognize spirit? The concept is prevalent in all human cultures and traditions. Spirit – what is it? I cannot answer this question. I can offer my perception that has come to me through observation, experience, study, contemplation, and meditation.

A few years ago, when I was first learning about spirituality, in conversation with my mentor, Rev. Patsy Walker Fine, I said that horses were as close as my breath. The words just slid out of my heart. Patsy's husband is a horseman, and we were discussing how, for the Tribe of Horse, a rider experiences their church on the back of a horse in nature. I was advocating her husband's point of view. When we are out in the natural world, we have a sense of awe. When we are horseback, we share our breath in the spiritual presence of Nature. I had no idea that what I intuitively spoke and felt, Horse as close as my breath, was backed up by etymology.

In most religious, folk, and spiritual traditions, the blending of Spirit and body giving rise to embodiment, takes place through the vehicle of the breath.

In many languages, the words for Spirit, soul, wind, and breath share the same etymology. (Mircea Eliade, Ed.

"Breath and Breathing," Encyclopedia of Religion, Vol. 2, pp. 302—304).

Are stories still written as they were when I became enamored of horse spirit — the stories of indomitable spirit and heart when Horse and Human were brought together in immense challenge and companionship — stories written by Marguerite Henry, Sam Savitt, Walter Farley, Will James, C.W. Anderson, and the all-time classic _Black Beauty_ by Anna Sewell?

Of course there are. Not just in children's books but also in adult reading. I am naming just a small sampling of great authors writing about Horse in fiction and nonfiction: Jane Smiley, Leanne Owens, Alan S. Evans, Mark Rashid, and Linda Kohanov. In 2002 we were entertained with the inspiring animated movie, a creation of DreamWorks, about the wild mustang, _Spirit: The Stallion of the Cimarron_, and his friendship with the American Indian, Little Creek. The animated horse character is based upon a Kiger Mustang who now resides at The Return to Freedom Horse Sanctuary in California. May 9, 2020, the Sanctuary celebrated his 25th birthday! Spirit is a real-life ambassador of Horse Spirit.

Spirit comes first. We just forget this in the process of learning the mechanics of tools and integrating tools with these sentient beings. We are the tool makers, we harness power with tools. And so, we learn about harnessing the power of horse with the implementation of halters, ropes, bits and bridles, saddles and cinches. Which bit do we use when, what saddle works best for the job at hand, how should weight be distributed? And the horse is to stand still while we work out the correct type and use of the tools we have created, until the horse itself becomes a tool to be manipulated. "Horses are just livestock," one person said to me.

Tom Dorrance, in his book *True Unity*, talks about what he calls a "third factor" when handling our horse — he names it *Spirit*.

> *I've been trying for some time to think of words to get this third factor to where it comes to light; to show how it blends in with the other two — physical and the mental. It is the least mentioned, but I am beginning to believe it is the most important factor to recognize: the rider needs to recognize the horse's need for self-preservation in Mind, Body and the third factor, Spirit.*

Once again we are looking to share the concept of unity and the state of being in which it is fostered and nurtured. We so often come to horses with the need to be right, the need to put our own agenda on the horse. It is our real job to leave the ego with our street clothes. When the riding clothes come on, we must abandon the mind-set of right and wrong, win or lose. I so often hear "you can't let the horse win." The horse has no conception of winning and losing. The horse is only trying to stay safe. If the horse "wins" her fight for self-preservation it is a lose-lose situation. The horse is not saying, "I won't do this at any cost." The horse is saying, "I don't understand what you want and why you are being so aggressive. You are frightening me. I just want to get away from you and the painful stuff you have put on me." It is our responsibility to come to the horse with a win-win proposition. Know what the horse needs. Know how to ask with the least amount of effort in a manner most natural to the horse's own communication skills.

Reading *Horse Sense and The Human Heart, What Horses Can Teach Us About Trust, Bonding, Creativity and Spirituality*, written by Adele von Rust McCormick, Ph.D. and Marlena Deborah McCormick, Ph.D., didn't change my consciousness of the Horse/Human relationship but validated it. In their introduction they write:

In our own interactions with horses we discovered a force — an unseen but ever-present energy that bathes the spirit and requires that we be completely present and true to our own nature. A horse's ability to connect with people is uncanny. Its size and presence somehow force us to become physically, mentally and spiritually more aware and more human. This elevated state of consciousness leads to renewed sensitivity and excitement, quite literally bringing us to our senses.

When we come to the horse with our senses open, our hearts open and our spirit seeking connection, we join the horse where Horse lives. In the mind's eye envision Horse, standing alert, head held high with nostrils flared, ears at attention. Hear her challenging snort. Feel her spirit expanding her heart, her lungs, and her body. What exquisite beauty and life essence. I am enlivened in spirit with every breath I share with her. This is what the horse invites me to embody. How awesome is that?

Heart

I am forever in awe of my first equine encounter. A white gelding is standing in his field, a magnet to my four-year-old heart. The power of his heart pulls me to him. I stand at the white board fence participating, with hopeful excitement, in his gentle approach. He lowers his great white head over the fence rail. Our breath intermingles, the whiskers on his chin tickle my child cheek. He allows and acknowledges the tentative touch of my child hand upon his muzzle. I was, I am, enchanted, enthralled, enamored.

What is this heartfelt phenomenon that we experience when we are sharing in the energy of Horse? For more than 27 years, the HeartMath Institute Research Center in Boulder Creek, CA, has explored the physiological mechanisms by which the heart and brain communicate and how the activity of the heart influences our perceptions, emotions, intuition, and health.

I was introduced to the ground-breaking studies of The HeartMath Institute at Sophia's Well, a Spiritual Wisdom Center in Sutter Creek, in the early part of my journey through the Ageless Wisdom Teachings. We learn from the wisdom teachings that the heart is an intelligent repository of wisdom, intuition, and knowingness; that it is connected to the brain, constantly informing our thoughts and emotions, of our inner resources and resonance. Our brains are so focused on the outer world and our outer senses that we rarely hear or listen to the whisperings of our heart.

Doc Childre and Howard Martin, with Donna Beech, have set forward in their book, _The HeartMath Solution_, a scientific presentation of the power of the heart in daily living. In a follow-up book, _The Science of the Heart_, we are given a comprehensive look at how the evolution of this new study of the heart/brain connection pervades all of our relationships, with ourselves, with other humans and creatures, and with the world at large. The following quotation is taken from _The Science of The Heart:_

In the early 1990s, we were among the first to conduct research that not only looked at how stressful emotions affect the activity in the autonomic nervous system (ANS) and the hormonal and immune systems, but also at the effects of emotions such as appreciation, compassion, and care. Over the years, we have conducted many studies that have utilized many different physiological measures... Consistently, however, it was heart rate variability (HRV), or heart rhythms, that stood out as the most dynamic and reflective indicator of one's emotional states and, therefore, current stress and cognitive processes... We also observed that the heart acted as though it had a mind of its own and could significantly influence the way we perceive and respond in our daily interactions. In essence, it appeared that the heart could affect our awareness, perceptions, and intelligence. Numerous studies have since shown that heart coherence is an optimal physiological state associated with increased cognitive function, self-regulatory capacity, emotional stability, and resilience.

So, what does this have to do with the Horse/Human relationship? In 2005, Ellen Kaye Gehrke, Ph.D., began a series of five studies to see if the HeartMath science would support using Heart Rate Variability (HRV) as a marker to demonstrate the emotional connection occurring between horses and humans when they interact. A description of these studies and findings are put forward in an extremely interesting and informative article, *The Horse-Human Heart Connection, Results of Studies Using Heart Rate Variability*, published in the Spring 2010 edition of The North American Riding for the Handicapped Association's publication, *STRIDES*.

The last of the five studies was conducted in 2008 in collaboration with Dr. Ann Baldwin, a physiologist from the University of Arizona. Using seven pairs of horses and humans as subjects, their study offered an interesting perspective on the Horse/Human relationship.

It appeared that each person synchronized his or her particular HRV frequency cycle to match the horse's specific frequency cycle. This result was reproducible and was observed in six out of the seven horse-human pairs. In the one horse-human pair in which the human did not match the horse's specific frequencies, the person stated that she was distracted with other responsibilities during the recording.

Dr. Gehrke enumerated several findings of interest in her article. The one that is most relevant to my "aha moment" states that:

Initial findings seem to reveal that the calmness or autonomic state of the horses has a greater influence on the human response rather than the other way around.

It is the heart resonance of the horse that influences humans. We are so often about us, how we influence our environment and our relationships, that we blind ourselves to the abounding energies that influence and flow through our lives. Horse heart entrains the human heart. Horse heart comes first.

I always ask my students why they want to learn to ride. The most common reply is, "I love horses." It is the love of horses that fuels the passion that drives a lifelong relationship with these magnificent creatures. With open heart we are enveloped by the wholeness felt in the presence of Horse. When we ride with our friends, we often share the idea that riding is more healing than therapy. I know a posse of women who have named their riding club "Group Therapy."

The biomagnetic power of that white gelding's great heart enveloped me all those years ago and has held me in embrace through all the journeys of my life.

Beauty

I am struggling with bringing Beauty out of the realm of the subjective, intuitional and metaphysical into objective, measurable and scientific concept. I am looking to validate the intrinsic beauty of Horse.

This search has brought me into the harmonizing concept of mathematics in nature, art, architecture and all things human, striving for rhythm and balance. Philosophers, scientists, artists, and theologians have all sought the paradigm of Beauty. Who am I, one small person in this great universal complex in which we reside, to take on the essence of Beauty? Because it is about Horse.

Beauty, it is said, is in the eye of the beholder. And yet the study of art and mathematics show there is a universal form to beauty — an asymmetrical balance that creates an ever-evolving movement, forever seeking to bring the whole into balance and forever recreating its asymmetry in a harmony that carries the eye into a mystery of searching. It is called the Golden Ratio, universal "sacred geometry" that shows itself in the spiral of galaxies, in the crest of an ocean wave, in the curves of a conch shell, and in the complex spiral of DNA. What is the Golden Ratio? So now I am going out on a limb, talking about mathematics, design, form and natural, organic beauty. Quite a combination of concepts.

Elaine J. Hom, *Live Science* contributer says:

The Golden Ratio is a special number found by dividing a line into two parts so that the longer part divided by the smaller part is also equal to the whole length divided by the longer part. It is often symbolized using phi, after the 21st letter of the Greek alphabet. In an equation form, it looks like this: a/b = (a+b)/a = 1.6180339887498948420 ...

Geometrically It looks like this:

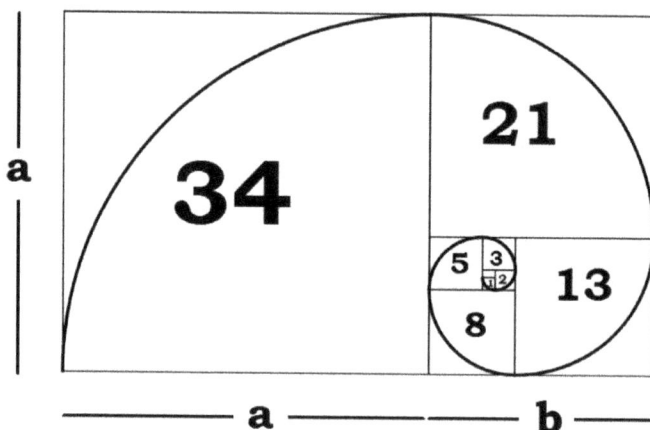

The artist, Diana Rueter-Twining, creates this vibrant beauty in her sculpture, allowing the essential horse energy to emerge through static form. Her wonderful creation, Maestro, is a perfect example of Horse in the potent balance of the Golden Ratio. She says of her process:

> *Dressage is a discipline of horse and rider requiring extreme strength, grace, balance and will. It is often associated with the famous white Lipizzaners of the Spanish Riding School in Vienna, Austria.*
>
> *I chose to pay homage to this in my sculpture, MAESTRO*. In studying the horse, I found that proportionally the horse in this gesture approximated the Golden Ratio or Divine Proportion in mathematics.*

16

"The outside of a horse is good for the inside of a man," is a famous quotation by Winston Churchill. Humans find beauty in a symmetry of proportion. Horse embodies the golden ratio many times over in its form. We can't help but admire the shape, the combination of curves and angles, the flare of nostrils, the flag of tail, the curtain of mane — beauty expressed in every part and every movement — universal, primordial beauty.

What is our human experience of Beauty? How do we recognize beauty? It is more than visual, it is visceral. Most of us are enamored of a beautiful sunset filled with color. We gaze at an artful rendering of the Mother and Child and feel a sense of loving awe. The greening of the hillsides and leafing of trees in spring after the naked winter always bring amazement and astonishment. The sparkling nighttime skyline view of San Francisco from across the bay is breath taking. Beauty takes us out of ourselves, absorbs us, nurtures our soul and spirit.

Horse beauty is a dynamic, living thing. It shines in the elegant cadenced choreography of the dressage horse, the classic curves of the Spanish horse, the crest of the wild mustang, the arc of the hunter over a fence, and the incredible athletic dance of the cutting horse. Horse is a universal symbol of free-flowing Beauty, Spirit, Courage and Freedom.

Beauty also comes in relationship, searching for that melding of Horse/Human understanding. As a teacher of foundational horsemanship, I ask my young students at their first lesson, "Why do you want to learn to ride a horse?" I have mentioned before the most common answer is, "I love horses." We can't go wrong with that. Starting from a place of love can only lead to success. For me, watching these young horse people struggle, trying to grasp the physical, mental, and emotional intricacies of learning to handle and ride a 1000-pound horse and then suddenly pushing past the barrier of not being able, to being able, is absolute beauty. I am passionate in sharing with these young people the experiences and practices that my more than half century of teaching has taught me. Yes, teaching teaches. My mentors teach me, the horses teach me, and students teach me. Learning reaches out through an entire lifetime; an intricate weaving of the interplay and continuity of sharing the Beauty of Horse.

Relationship

Relationship – That mystical third thing when two come together. Everything, everywhere, is in relationship. Think about it.

Horses are all about relationship. They are constantly aware of each other, of their placement in their herd, and the space and environment around and about them. For horses it is about survival. They are hypervigilant of the intent and emotion of all the beings that surround them. Horse knows that all is connected.

Humans, on the other hand, are about separateness, the individual focused on herself. Humans are goal oriented, living in their thoughts rather than their bodies, their group, their environment. A good example of this single focus is our current lack of relationship with our environment and how it is affecting the planet and our lives.

I was thirteen years old when horses came into my daily life. I was deeply enamored of these wonderful creatures and sponge-learned their habits and behavior. I watched and compared my book learning with the horses' interactions, their body language and facial expressions. I soaked up the words of the adults that were the authority. We had two gentle mares, quintessential kid horses, that taught us the beginning language of horsemanship. These horses carried us with good humor and waited patiently for us when we dropped off their backs.

The two horses lived together, one black named Dilly, and one bay named Mazie, in the neighborhood horse facility that our fathers built. They had to be fed separately because the bay horse would chase the black horse from her food with bared teeth and threatening hooves. One day, for a reason long forgotten, Dilly was tied to the tree that grew in the middle of the corral. Mazie, literally, attacked her, kicking and kicking with a ferocity that was stunning to my young heart and mind. I was finally able to chase the bay mare away. The black mare was unharmed. These same mares, when separated, would pace, fret, and whinny until the other horse returned. No matter what I did to try and replace the separation the mare felt, she would not be consoled. Even food distracted her for just a moment.

I learned a big lesson in relationship and horse behavior. First, my love for these horses did not, in any way shape or form, alter their natural equine behavior. Second, never put a horse in a position where it cannot defend itself. Third, horses can give and take physical contact that can mortally injure a human.

One horse that came into our sphere was a proud-cut gelding, a horse whose testicles had not been completely removed and were still making testosterone. He collected those mares, made them his, and then chased us kids out whenever we came into his "territory." He did not stay long, but again we learned a new dynamic in relationship. We were kicked out of our own space. I learned respect for the power of Horse "dark side." Stallions in the wild will fight to the death for herd leadership, and then the victorious stallion may kill any foals that are not his. This aggressive display of herd dynamics in our home "herd" did not last more than a week. The horse disappeared as he had appeared, outside of our influence. There was an adult orchestrater behind the scenes.

These are the more dramatic of my youthful learning experiences, the 'off side' examples. The 'near side', the side that we tend to want to see, the essence of love and sensitivity, include visions of a pinto pony mare licking and encouraging her newborn foal, a twitch of a brown coated muscle dislocating a fly, and a soft, gentle muzzle nuzzling the palm of my hand for offered oats.

As a prey animal, Horse is always aware of his environment. Horse tastes, smells, and listens to the messages brought on the breeze. His eyesight is almost a full 360-degree circle with his only blind spots directly in front and behind him. Hooves instinctively lash out in a protective kick when a horse is startled from behind. Horse muzzle is so sensitive he can separate medicated powder from grain. Every time we are with Horse, our senses expand through his. Horse and Human are always in a two-way conversation if we listen, watch, and be fully in the presence of Horse.

I came to "Natural Horsemanship" when the relationship with my beloved Sandman broke down. He was the horse of my dreams, a lovely gelding that I had raised from conception to be my dressage horse. There were too many holes in my knowledge and awareness of the Horse/Human relationship. Working full time, supporting my family of husband, three children, and assorted animals, I lost the sense of the time necessary to properly move through the learning levels my colt needed to safely take on a rider. I forgot two things; two days a week, even though it felt to me like just yesterday, are not enough to instill the lessons taught. And more importantly, to always have my horse's eye on me. Where his eye and ear goes, his attention goes. I stepped into the stirrup for the first time and my colt leaped out from under my precarious balance, the surprise of my weight seeming to come out of nowhere. On landing I cracked my elbow and my confidence. I realized I needed help.

A new trainer, Anne Soule, had come into our community. A young, lithe, athletic woman, she spoke to a horse on a level that mirrored my image of a true horseperson. She had studied with the top Horsemanship Clinicians of the time, from the Classical tradition of the Old World to the New World style of the Vaquero. She offered training from the perspective of the horse and horse behavior. A new level of learning the Horse/Human relationship began for me, and it has never stopped.

Church of the Round Pen, A Study in Relationship

Let me retouch the joy I felt working and playing with the beautiful mare, Chloe, as we became acquainted in a Bear Valley Springs round pen. Let me share the joyous sense of communion found in balancing energy between horse and human. I am visiting my brother, just outside of Tehachapi, California. He has two very nice horses: Silver, a gentle giant, half shire-half quarter horse gelding, a delightful silver grey, and he has Chloe, feminine, lovely, elegant, half Friesian-half Paint, a beautiful balance of black and white. I am smitten with her.

Chloe and I don't know each other, I have been told she has a certain level of training. I find when I ask her to move up to that level she is confused, not sure as to how to respond, and becomes agitated, throwing more and more energy into escaping my request. I lift my energy, changing my body posture to more assertive as she escalates. I know that somewhere she knows the correct response, and I wait for her to find it, not letting up on my response to the energy she is throwing out. And suddenly she finds it, bending her ear and eye to me. Her head and tail lower, she begins to respond rather than react, and I yield the pressure of my energy. She begins to lick her lips. I am joyful in our communication. We have found a momentary balance, a balance to build upon.

We see the round pen, a simple 40' to 60' diameter enclosure, as a place of schooling for the horse; but in reality, hidden in plain sight, is the dance of relationship, the coming together of energies, enfolding one into the other, creating a communication of mind, body, and spirit. Horse spirit is our captivator. We are enthralled with the primordial, free expression of horse in body and action. We want to capture that spirit and make it our own. Of course, we can't capture it; we can only interface with it, come to that common denominator that enlivens each of us.

Like any church, the round pen practice can be misinterpreted to be all about dogma and rules. Rules are guide posts to a deeper entanglement of promise and potential. When we bind ourselves to rules, we bind ourselves to the structure of ego. Ego structure is important, and when used positively, it is a portal to the greater dimension of energetic relationship. If used in its negative aspect, it becomes an impassable boundary.

This is deep stuff, and I don't mean to scare anybody away. We, of The Tribe of Horse, all seek that mystic relationship with our horse, the relationship where we become one in mind, body, and spirit.

Horse, Heroes and Archetypes

I grew up with larger than life, silver screen horse heroes. The horses, not the men that rode them, were my heroes. In retrospect, it was the relationship between the man and his horse, true partners of mutual respect and understanding, which inspired my admiration. In almost every origin story, the horse of untamable spirit is rescued by the hero. With tenderness and compassion the hero wins the power of the horse spirit. The horse is still wild but has given, without coercion, his loyalty to the hero, thus transforming the two into one for the highest good. WOW! My heart wanted the same communion with Horse that was shared by Silver and The Lone Ranger, Trigger and Roy Rogers, and Champion and Gene Autry.

Some might say that this Horse/Human relationship is Hollywood fiction, but if you were to ask any person that relies on a horse for their life or livelihood the answer would be that this is real. Every passionate horse person feels this relationship in their core. It is the archetype of the hero, the hero's journey and the horse as guide, strength, power conductor, and partner. It is about transforming the limited human reality into having all of our assets of an apex earth-energy animal, body and spirit.

The legend of Alexander the Great and his taming of the magnificent Bucephalus is well known among the Tribe of Horse. The stallion was brought before the King, Alexander's father, by a horse trader offering to sell the horse for an exorbitant amount of money. The giant black horse, though beautiful, was unrideable, and so the King was not interested. Alexander, then only 12 or 13 years old, said he would ride the stallion and if he was thrown, he would pay the money for the horse himself. On approaching Bucephalus Alexander saw that the horse was shying from his own shadow. Talking softly and turning the black into the sun, Alexander removed his flapping cape and stood silently and soothingly in presence with the horse. The horse quieted and Alexander vaulted upon his broad back and together they galloped towards the sun. The rest is history.

Walter Farley published his now classic book, *The Black Stallion,* in 1941. It is a modern rendition of the ancient story of Bucephalus and Alexander. The myth was beautifully recreated for the silver screen in 1979 by Francis Ford Coppola. This is a harrowing adventure of life and death, resurrection, and transformation. The bigger-than-real-life hero's journey. Those of us who grew up on *The Black Stallion* series couldn't help but be enthralled with this masterful, artistic reenactment of everything that is challenging, beautiful and rewarding in this magical Horse/Human relationship.

The awesome reality is that this relationship is not magic. Each of us, if we take the time to understand Horse nature and behavior, to honor it and practice the tools of communication that are offered everywhere we look these days: at clinics, in instructional DVDs, and books, can have this beautiful bond with our horses. Like anything worthwhile, it is time consuming, arduous, and to be practiced with patience and love. A passion to share in the presence of these wonderful animals is a prerequisite. In order to harness the archetypal energy of Horse, we must come with humility, understanding, timelessness, honesty, and willingness to relate from the place that is the being of the Horse.

Just as there are the Ageless Wisdom Teachings for Humanity so there is for the Horse/Human relationship. The Art of Horsemanship was written in year 350BC by the Greek historian, philosopher, soldier, and horseman, Xenophon, laying a foundation of knowledge and communication skills that would be lost and rediscovered over the centuries. And he was not the first to put this wisdom into written words.

So, what is an archetype and what is the archetype of Horse as it relates to the members of The Tribe of Horse?

Horse as archetype is often described as untethered power of emotion, primal instinct and energy of the unconscious. Horse is also considered a bridge between spirit and matter, incorporating both in its relationship with Human. In mythology horses pulled the chariot of the sun when handled with care and respect, but they brought the chariot and sun crashing to the earth when misused in ignorance, causing great damage to the world. Horse has been an integral partner with humanity for so long we forget and take for granted the essence of that partnership.

When I was a tween, I would pretend to be a horse. I say pretend, but what I really mean is I would become my image of a horse, unbridled power and freedom in physicality. I became the joy that I saw in a horse galloping in abandon across an openness that was bounded only by the horizon. Sitting in meditation today I sought expression for Lynnea's Horse path. My image was of her held and carried by the undulating power of Horse.

What began intuitively in play became a life long Journey with Lynnea the Hero and Horse the Archetype of Power, Speed, Passion, and Nature Essence — guide to the conscious connection of mind, body, emotion and spirit. It is the human journey of awakening to consciousness.

In youth the connection is fluid, free, and unfettered. Lynnea moved into the wholeness of herself when in the presence and on the back of Horse. Without Horse she was separate, unformed, awkward, self-conscious.

In motherhood Lynnea formed a bond with her children that changed her relationship with Horse. Lynnea forgot her deep connection to horse in the primal protection of her children and herself as a mother. Knowing the vulnerability of her children she recognized the vulnerability in herself. Horse, now in its archetype manifestation, began to show the shadow side of itself, powerfully dangerous with an aura of stampeding emotions and spirit.

Yet the passion for the journey with Horse remained. Step-by-step, the relationship was rebuilt in a new level of awareness. A gentle black mare, named Chipeta, guided Lynnea back to knowing the generous gift of heart, and the consistency of personality and performance that Horse offers. She reminded Lynnea that the foundation for harmonious relationship was still available. There was so much to learn.

The mythic ride continued in humility, coming to the horse from a different perspective. This was not about Lynnea and Horse, but about Horse and Lynnea. Of course, it had always been that, but a new level of respect was introduced. A new level of learning was required. An eclectic education led to dressage tests, Trail Trials, barrel racing, playing over crossed and layered poles, driving in harness, endurance rides, and the awesome natural backdrop of trails ridden from the Lost Coast of California to the Pacific Crest Trail on top of mighty Sierra Nevada Mountains.

Mentoring from Masters, Study, Practice, Service, and The Golden Rule guide the student through the wisdom teachings and the archetype hero's journey. Challenge is met first with unknowing, then seeking knowledge and direction, perfecting that learning, using it to reach the goal, then helping others on the path. Lynnea returned home to her heart in Horse, sharing her passion and hard-won skill with those that came to her for guidance.

The Tribe of Horse

A young, budding horsewoman introduced me to the concept of The Tribe of Horse. I was offering pony rides with my mighty Miniature Horse, Shadow, at the local Farmer's Market held in our small Sierra Foothill town. She came to ride, telling me that she was from the Tribe of Horse. Of course she was, and in that moment, I realized I too was a member of the Tribe of Horse.

Who are these people that comprise The Tribe of Horse? Oxford Dictionary defines "tribe" as *a social division in a traditional society consisting of families or communities linked by social, economic, religious, or blood ties, with a common culture and dialect, typically having a recognized leader.* The recognized leader in the Tribe of Horse is, of course, Horse.

Each of us has our own emotional, physical, and mental blueprint. In esoteric philosophy this is known as the etheric or energy body. We each have our own relationship foundation with Horse. Where one horseperson may cover 100's of miles in competitive endurance riding, sharing the challenges of horsemanship, endurance, and environment in extreme trail conditions, another horseperson may find complete satisfaction in day to day conversations in the corral, brushing, feeding, caregiving, with never the need to mount the horse. Each is in relationship with the horse, spending time in communion with a being of infinite presence.

It is joy, mystery and awe that lead into the Tribe of Horse. Once there the instruction is rigorous, with mental, emotional, and physical challenges, the humps, bumps and falls of life reflected in the microcosm of the Horse/Human relationship. Our guide is a child of this earth, a cauldron of earth energy, powerful in all its aspects.

I was blessed with the opportunity to attend, as an auditor in the stands, two clinics with the legendary Tom Dorrance. I can't say I came away with specific training techniques, the scope and shape of communication was too subtle – what I did witness was a man of infinite compassion grounded in the knowledge of compassionate connection on a level few humans ever attain.

I first heard of Ray Hunt back in the early 70s – A man who spoke to the nature of the horse. I remember thinking, "Wow, it's about time." Little did I know this was the birth of "Natural Horsemanship," and a level of communication between horse and human being brought to the national and international horse community in a new teaching forum known as "The Clinic." This great horseman did more for the horse than any "Trainer" before. I was privileged to watch him teach 30 years later.

As a teacher I pass on my knowledge with my heart and soul. I find I tune in with every fiber of my being in the attempt to communicate and share my knowledge, described in the clumsiness of words. When I connect with a young person who grasps intuitively the concepts of the Horse/Human relationship connection, it is a joyful experience. It is impossible for me to not become very attached to these kids. I watch them with nurturing eye and hand, grow as horse people. I see them explore, get stuck, experience the light of understanding, and I move through all of this with them. It is personally fulfilling and rewarding. However, I know with every lesson, every interaction, there will come a day for them to spread their wings and move on to the next level, the next horsemanship experience, the next expansion of their passion…the passion that we share. They will leave me. Which is what the preparation is all about. It is one of the goals of the teaching. I am devastated, inconsolable, just like a parent whose children have left home.

I have to say, there is real wonder in Facebook. A woman found me, a woman that I knew briefly when she was a youngster and I wasn't much older. I have been following her postings and page. She now owns a Thoroughbred Bloodstock farm in Florida. I mentioned to her how wonderful it was that she has fulfilled the horsewoman's dream. She responded that I was responsible. WOW. What a gift she gave me in those few words. This sharing of the passion for horses has been going on for more than fifty years. It isn't only in this moment. Just as there are people that have helped me along this journey, the ones I think of in gratitude, Del Gonzales, Andy Ruiz, and Anne Soule, there are those whose lives I have touched. We are all linked in this love of horses.

I can release my kids, with love, to their future and their past. I go with them in their journey. I am so grateful that, as a member of the Tribe of Horse, I have the gift of sharing the passion for these incredible creations of God, the Horse. In the end, it is all about our horses.

Part Two
Poetry

A Wonderful Sensual Life

The Maiden and the Unicorn

This poem honors that first encounter, my first meeting with a horse. My grandfather cleaned pools in Palm Springs. When I visited my grandparents, he would sometimes take me along with him to a job. This white horse was next door to where he was working, and under a watchful eye, he let me go to see the horse. I don't really remember her, but I know there was a woman present. She told me the horse's name was King. I do remember King had black speckles around his eyes and his muzzle. His nostrils were pink. It was 1951.

The girl child's
Body presses
Against white board fence,
Leans into the
Presence of Horse.
His great white head
Drops to her side.
She is still.
His breath tickles
The soft baby hair of her cheek.
His eye comes level with hers,
And in that moment
A mystic exchange is made.
His milk chocolate eye
Melts into her heart,
Mystery, adventure, surrender;
The connection of Maiden and Unicorn.

Sensuous Life — *"When I was a girl I would roam through the pastures with my horse, Spotty, and there would be a communion, a great sensuous song of life being sung through us that I have no words for." Anonymous*

These words are so very validating to read, the experience similar to my own. It is only as I grow in years and wisdom that I truly acknowledge the communion with nature, with life, that riding my horse has granted me: A blessing of spirit, "a great sensuous song of life...." Several years ago, I attempted to put this wondrous song into a poem.

Meadow Music – A Rider's Song

Meadow music notes of spring
Flow the contour of the hills
Swirl the ponderosa canyons
To the rhythm of gentle hoof beats walking
To the meadow music notes of spring.
Yellow flowers rising, reaching sunburst beauty
To the gentle hoof beats passing through their midst
Walking gentle hoof beats,
One-two, one-two, one-two-three-four.
Meadow grass seeds on their slender stalks
Bow and bob in unison to the rhythm of
The meadow music notes of spring
To the gentle rhythmic hoof beats
Of the mare walking in the horse dimension.

Meadow music notes of summer
Simmer warmly through the valley
Wrap round trails traced on hillsides

To the rhythm of muffled hoof beats walking
To the meadow music notes of summer.
Powder puffs of cedar scented dust rise in rhythm
To the muffled hoof beats passing on the path.
Walking muffled hoof beats,
One-two, one-two, one-two-three-four.
Toasted gold by summer solstice
The meadow grass sways in sleepy melody to
The meadow music notes of summer
To the muffled rhythmic hoof beats
Of the mare walking in the horse dimension.

Meadow music notes of autumn
Serenade the oaks and alder,
Decked in glowing passion colors,
To the rhythm of happy hoof beats walking
To the meadow music notes of autumn.
Leaves red and gold shake and shimmy
To happy hoof beats walking in their glory.
Happy walking hoof beats,
One-two, one-two, one-two-three-four.
Parading the yellow-leafed road,
Petals of sunlight flutter and fall to
The meadow music notes of autumn
To the gentle rhythmic hoof beats
Of the mare walking in the horse dimension.

Meadow music notes of winter
Sing the blackbirds in the choir loft
Of the ancient oak tree's branches
To the rhythm of crisp hoof beats walking

To the meadow music notes of winter.
Five hundred voices trilling, singing gospel in god's house
To crisp hoof beats passing 'neath their perch.
Crisp walking hoof beats,
One-two, one-two, one-two-three-four.
In the waning light of winter, reflected in the shivering pond,
Barren branches nod to the rhythm of
The meadow music notes of winter
To the crisp rhythmic hoof beats
Of the mare walking in the horse dimension.

There is such a deep, emotional satisfaction in watching a child interact with a horse. To see the very moment when the child's body and mind begin to synchronize with the movement of the horse, to synchronize with the rhythm, lift and sway of this huge energetic bundle of muscle and nerve, is always astoundingly beautiful.

Beauty

Six months past
Was her lesson last.
A nine-year-old
Seeking the elusive gold,
A treasure so bold,
A story retold.
The joining of beings,
The vistas of seeings
From the back of a horse,
A bridge to the source
Of nine-year-old glory,
An adventure story.
She sits astride a gentle ride,
The fat round mare
Of snow-white hair.
She listens with care,
Words her teacher shares.
Her body tries so hard to do
What her teacher says is true.
Try as hard as she may
Her seat just won't stay
In the saddle so wide

And the bouncy stride
Jars her seat from the saddle.
To stay on is a battle.
"Sure can't chase cattle
If you can't stay astraddle,"
Teacher says from the center,
The words of her mentor.
Clasping hard on the reins,
Child's hand jerks and strains.
Back, rubber band bending,
Mixed messages she's sending.
The teacher does muse
What words can she choose?
So child's seat she won't lose,
This young psyche won't bruise.
Teacher calls on her knowing
To lead to the flowing
Of harmony felt
When two bodies melt
Into exquisite rhythm
And shared body wisdom.
"Imagine head lifting high,
A string attached to sky,
Your breathe a soft sigh,
Your legs a draped "Y"
Across horse's back,
Over horse tack,
Legs stretching down,
Heels reaching for ground,
Hands push against bounce,
Weighing only an ounce,

Seat pumps like a swing
So that you won't fling
Off from the spring
When the horse is trotting."
And then it is there,
As though from thin air.
Little body is straight
And in rhythm with gait,
Hands float above wither
Like the play of a zither.
Fingers fold 'round rein
So as not to cause pain.
Soft, without strain.
It has not been in vain
This effort of love — A gift from above
This moment of Beauty, A Rider, A Cutie.

I am a horsewoman, not a cowgirl. Cattle have been a part of the landscape for most of my adult life and I love that landscape. I have had the delightful experience of interacting with cattle, on horseback, two handfuls of times. Horse owns my Heart.

Horse Gal

From the back of a horse I've trailed a
Cow for maybe a couple of miles.
To call me a cowgirl can only
Engender a few derisive smiles.

From the back of a horse I've trailed the
Miles of soul song, youth and years.
To call me a horse gal is close to the
Truth agreed upon by my peers.

For a horse is my expression of Life,
Life's Art for it's very own sake
In harmony with body, soul, and mind,
Spirit Guide to God's Heavenly gate.

The high flash of hooves, fire flicked mane,
Horse emotions are bold and brave.
Horse lifts me out of my narrow world
And carries me to a land without grave.

My buckskin mare in gentle embrace
Wraps her neck around my breast.
I scratch her ear, give thanks for our
Rides, and know that I am blessed.

My friend, Ingrid, and I came to horses at the same time, sharing a neighborhood experience, a gathering of girls in their early teens, fulfilling the dream of having horses. This poem was a birthday present to my life-long friend. It honors the gift of her sharing her piece of heaven with me.

Her Piece of Heaven

Wind sounds eternal on the flat,
Shifting shape of Juniper and Sage,
Flutter, flatten, sway and rage
Through the eons to this age.
We sit and feel the pulse of sound
Rock the motorhome against the ground.
Listen to the spirit seeking passage 'round
The slender walls, beneath, above, bound
Forever on its journey 'cross the plain,
Cradled in the mighty mammoth mountain range.
We listen, my friend of fifty years and I.

Morning's doorway opens the new day,
Beckons our excitement to embrace
This brilliant and illuminated space
Framed by the high-ridged mountain face.
Horses fresh and fed reluctantly stand
To be saddled with the skill of practiced hand.
Our route is carefully planned
To breathe this view of heaven's magic land.
Mounted on my life friend's horse,
Cradled in the mighty mammoth mountain range,
We ride, my friend of fifty years and I.

41

Traversing the mountain trails chiseled
Long ago by mules' hooves and miners' booted feet,
Saddles rock in rhythm to our horses' hoof beat
Eternal echo of our own harmonic heartbeat,
Mirror of the mountain's molten spirit
Lifted through the lava spire summit
Piercing clouds and sky it hides its secret,
Spoken only in the sound of wind and creek and granite.
Memory making, mounted horseback,
Cradled in the mighty mammoth mountain range,
We share, my friend of fifty years and I.

Humbled and inspired we bid our ride goodnight.
We cuddle into covers, warm with wine and conversation
Listening to Dave Stamey's cowboy song creation
Of romance between the horse and human nation.
We laugh with chick flick Mama Mia, voices lifted upward,
Nostalgia current in the confines of communion inward,
Times of love, birth and death whispered heart-ward,
Wind outside the walls, horses huddled rear-ward.
My friend shares with me her piece of heaven,
Cradled in the mighty mammoth mountain range
We are, my friend of fifty years and I.

"Anne" honors the woman that opened a new dimension in the relationship I have shared with Horse. I am forever grateful.

Anne

You came into my world hardly noticed.
Horsemen's conversation brought you into focus.
It was said there was a trainer (an archaic label not expressive of your skill)
Who understood and spoke to the nature of a horse,
Who went beyond mechanics of control and constriction,
Who spun the kaleidoscopic spirits of Horse and Human
Into a united spirit of harmony and rhythm.
You stood there tall and competent
When I came to you with shattered ego and crumbling confidence.
You took my insecure reactive colt and my insecure reactive self
And taught us the language of horse and handler.
You offered us the knowledge necessary to
Create the communion shared by horse and woman.
Your teaching allowed me to regain my youthful dream,
The quest for the perfect partnership, myself and my horse
Melding into one harmonious being, body and spirit,
Riding the wind, cresting the ocean's curl, leaping the moon.
Your teaching allowed the possibility of realizing that dream.
You embody the horsewoman I envisioned as the potential in myself.

I have been blessed to share my life with many horses. Sparkle has been with me since she was a sparkle in her parents' eyes. It had not been my intention to keep her. I thought she was too small. Anne, after spending a few days with her in initial under-saddle training, said, "She is a keeper." Sparkle's heart shines with the sunshine that brings blossoming life after spring rain.

Sparkle Plenty

My horse is
the concrete connection
to the abstract
of my soul.
Like Pegasus flying
Icarus to the sun
she carries me
to the outreaches of my world,
dropping piles of care and concern along the way.
She is Sparkle Plenty,
namesake to the beautiful Bad girl
in the Dick Tracey comic strip.
Even as a newborn foal
life poured from her like sunrays.
The genetics of grey bring the glitter
of diamond dust to her shiny coat.
Her ears stand sentinel straight
when she hears my call
and she answers me with
a joyful welcome whinny.
Like me she has some arthritis,
some wisdom and some silliness.

Time and a well-lived life take their toll. I willingly pay the price of the toll.

Turn Back the Hands of Time

I'd like to be out riding with my friends today
But something came along and took that life away.
From my deck I watch my mare talking to the wind
Restlessly walking the grazed confines of her pen.
The wind beckons us to chase her breath across the hills.
To once again trace well-loved trails, to leave behind the pills.
She trumpet snorts and beckons me, this old gray mare of
mine.
Come, let us join the wild wind's call, turn back the hands of
time.

There is never too much to say about the Love of Horse

Writing about Horse

Horses are eternal
Sparkle Plenty
Soul Joy

What more can I say?
Every time I see
Her happy expectation,
Head high, ears at attention,
Eyes gleaming, body poised,
My heart leaps out to her
In gratitude so great
I am eternally astounded.

Legs lifted in joyous canter,
Mane tossed and tumbled in jubilation,
Neigh trumpeted in bouncing bravado,
She is a horse.
Fluid and flying
Feet dancing down the dusty drive
Of the home where she was born
So many years before.
Now transforming into wild mare
Galloping with her herd
In the expression of primal freedom.

I wonder?

Silver Hair

What do people think
As they drive by the pasture
Where my horses' dwell
And see a silver-haired woman
Clad in shorts and tank top
Sitting astride a silver-haired horse?
My old mare and I
Move across the dry pasture,
She balancing me so effortlessly,
Me riding her happy rhythm,
Enjoying each other's company,
In the way of well-known friends.
Do people see the crippling
Of aged bones,
Of vulnerability,
That once was
A Sense of Pure
Whole body Exuberance?

In the Ageless Wisdom Teachings, we learn about Ethical Living and the Virtues. We use the practice of seed-thought meditation. We take a virtue and spend a month unpacking the nuance of meaning. I have attempted to bring the idea of virtue into the Horse/Human relationship. Reverence is about coming from a place of humility in the heart.

Reverence

With reverence my hand and brush
Trace the arc of her neck, the swell of her wither,
The dip of her back, the rounding of rump,
Lifting earth debris from the infinite of hairs
That cover her in golden glory.

With reverence I look into her amber eye,
Searching for the primordial life and spirit
Captured there,
But only see a reflection of light and dark
Protecting the mystery of her soul.
With reverence I honor her sharing
In the inflection of her ear,
The blow of her nostrils,
The flick and lift of tail hairs,
The softening of her eye.

In reverence I acknowledge that space in me she opens,
That awareness of spirit and energy
That is present in the moment, in the space we inhabit.
Her sensitivity extends my senses into the space
I cannot see, but only feel, intuit. Mystery.

We talk a lot about the role of Leadership in the Horse/Human dance. Leadership is one of the Virtues to be seriously contemplated.

Leadership

You lead me — I lead you.
I lead you into my human creation of ego, self, and personal needs.
You lead me into connection, unity, wordless communication, nature- energy.
I lead you into the corral, barn, arena, horse-trailer.
You lead me into bird song, laughing spring water, spired forests, endless horizons.
I lead you with constraint of halter and rope, with goal intention.
You lead me with a promise of filling this primal yearning that permeates my being.
I lead you with my dreams, my heart, and my highest intention.
You lead me into my dreams, my heart, and my highest intention.
You follow me in acceptance and affection.
I follow you in passion and love.

Transformation is all about growth to a higher perspective. Horse offers the image of transformation in her actions, behavior, and attitude. Meg offered me the experience of Transformation generously and often.

Transformation

Today we made thunder – You made thunder.
I am the witness making the space available.
You are my horse, the primal voice of my passion.
Lightning lanced, you arc and lash and flare.
A tornado tossed tumbleweed, your buckskin body
Bounds, lifts, floats, and dances in
The theater of the round pen
to the strident concussion of your own music.
I stand in the eye of your storm,
Reveling in the power of your expression,
tasting the turbulent wind funneled through your nostrils
vibrating to the pounding rhythm your
hooves drum on the skin of sod and soil.
And then the storm is spent.
Your canter is cradle rocking soft,
A Soul soothing cadence quiet as an April shower.
I lift my hand and step back, a beckoning bow
Inviting you to share the center with me.
You come, ears up, muzzle reaching into my cupped hands,
You blow a gentle Zephyr, the west wind's promised warmth.
The scent of exuberant exertion lifts off your body, damp and dense.
You are Life coming to me willingly,
 You share your heart space.

Part Three
Horse as Muse — Journal Writing

4/09/08 — I am off to play horse. I think Pat Parelli said that, play with your horse, don't work with him. That lifted such a weight off me...a weight of perfectionism, ambition, and self-motivation. It became about me and the horse together, play — a communication game, charades. She would say, "Hi, should I be happy to see you? Do you have a carrot or a saddle?"

Her ears up, her eyes bright, her nose touches my hand. "Today I have a carrot and a saddle," I answer. I slip the halter strap over her neck; she pushes her nose through the nose loop; I knot the halter and offer the carrot in the flat of my palm. I might have answered, "Today I have a carrot and a connection."

No halter, I offer the carrot in the flat of my hand, run my hands on the fullness of her neck and along her back, the roundness of her rump, and scratch her belly. "Oh, that feels soooo gooood," she says, stretching her neck and wiggling her lips. I love to play with my horse, to carry on a nurturing conversation. Of course, just like in any close relationship, we are not always so perfectly attuned to each other.

04/25/08 — My back is sore but okay today — so much fear of pain. Yesterday was amazing. I trotted next to Meg, hanging onto her side. I felt my fear, the stiffness in her left side, the tightness in my back. When she blasted past me, I didn't shatter, she didn't explode. I let her go. Before too many blasts, I realized we were okay and I could reach out and communicate that I needed/wanted her to go slower — a shake of the lead rope and she adjusted her pace to mine. In the end, my breath gave out before my body.

I watched Anne transform before my eyes — at will filling her body with powerful energy. Meg, standing next to her, responded with ears pricked, watchful, waiting. Is it age that wants me to stay in its old comfort zone? Do I have that energy to bring up for my horse, or have I spent it all on Bob and just want to plunk and futz with my horses? That's how it feels. Stepping out into training again takes a focused energy.

I wish Anne would tell me when I am over reactive. Meg turned away from me, and I lashed out towards her with the tail of the rope. I was irritated by her lack of respect, not staying with me until I released her. I think I need a release cue like I have with the dogs. Now I feel guilty.

4/26/08 — I am taking a walk with my Australian Shepherd, Zack, and my Shi-Tzu, Macho Man. My neighbor has a couple of horses in the pasture next to the dirt road I am following. He is out with the horses, and we start talking. He says about the bay gelding standing near the fence, "He doesn't like men, but for the kids, he comes up and lets them put the halter on. This old gelding carries four or five kids at a time. I'll be leading him and he'll stop. I look back and the kids are listing off to one side. That horse won't move until the kids are up there in the middle of his back. How they know about kids, I don't know."

Which got me to thinking: We know about babies of all species. Why shouldn't they? How often are geldings used as horse babysitters? My Miniature horse gelding played Uncle to my big horse filly. A very special bond they formed. My old palomino mare would drop her head and soften her eye whenever a child approached. My gray mare is not so nurturing. She wrinkles her nose at the kids. She knows they are not her peers.

7/23/10 — There is a tsunami of joy and exaltation coming — giant-crested with an ocean of galloping horses, manes lifted on arched necks, nostrils snorting sea foam, eyes glistening sunlight sparks, legs thrashing the waves, pounding the shore with the thunder of storm-clashed curls, hurling against my heart and soul, lifting and carrying me in the triumphant energy. It is the ride of my Life, filled with Holy Spirit, Horse Spirit, Mystery — knowledge of our sacred place on Earth.

7/26/10 — Tears of gratitude embrace my heart and Remedy's gift. The gift of giving and the drive to understand. A delving into mystery, handing her my heart and having it returned to me fuller for the giving. She has a major brace in her neck, tense high-headedness. I hope to help her release that tension and know how much better she can feel when she lowers her head, not in submission, but in harmony with the balance of her body. Exercises that I know may help to bring this about: gait transitions, emotional transitions. As she learns to move more smoothly through her gait transitions, she learns to accept her emotion and does not need to elevate them to move with more energy. Poll and jaw relaxation, dropping her head, all resistance-lowering movements.

8/5/10 — A Point of Teaching: In teaching horsemanship we teach love: understanding, unity, and consciousness, awareness of both our own motives and the sentient other of the horse. We teach and learn the dynamics of divinity (as I currently understand divinity).

8/11/10 — It is a bit difficult to draw a comparison of Horse as a guide to God when I am reading that this entire world and everything in it is a dream, an illusion. However, I think I see a correlation. As a child, with the perception of youth, horses were my dream. I read horse stories, educational horse books, played with imaginary horses from Breyer to a wooden barrel on sawhorses. I became a horse, snorting, galloping, neighing in freedom. When I purchased my first horse, Champagne blended her body with mine, I blended my mind with hers. She gave me power to move through the chaotic emotional years growing up in a difficult family. She was refuge, expression, passion, and acceptance of blossoming body. She accommodated all the states of mind and emotion, the perception of knowing myself, making myself okay with my dream, my life as I understood it.

11/1/10 — A Point of Teaching: We always greet our horse with welcome and love. You must remember that she is a living, feeling being, just like you. She just perceives the world differently than you. Imagine a fawn in the woods, curled in her bed of pine needles or oak leaves, keeping still as her mother has advised. She is prey to coyote, wolf, and cougar. She is fearful but safe as long as she does what her mother tells her. This is the world in which horses live. A world where she must stay safe from predators — things that may eat her. So, from the very beginning, we bring our loving energy to her.

Contemplation

As we spend time in each other's company, we share and extend — relate on a level of emotion and energy. Horses are highly sensitive to the emotional environment (the astral level). We learn to influence through understanding horse nature.

11/18/10 — Helping Pete find his way into the open stall, working in harmony with Meg Verardi, was an experience in communion. I have a friend to share the horseback dance with — we are on the same level. We worked together without external direction. Our direction came from Pete: He was the conductor and the orchestra. We were the stage and the instruments. His fear of stepping over the lip of the board into the shadowed space sent tremors across his skin. His resistance was based on something we could not know but was very real to him — perhaps failing eyesight.

12/28/10 — What fun to create a space that is dedicated to the horse. It seems we have come full circle as Horse in human society is once again a psychological-spiritual bridge to the metaphysical world. Through music, art, and words, we reach for that liberation of being that flows through and is represented in horse anatomy and being. I wish I could capture the essence in words. Seeing Ruth's painting of Mystery inspired me. Ruth is an artist, a neighbor, and a horse lover. She created a life-size painting of her black horse, Mystery, standing at rest — an artistic representation of Horse mystery.

1/3/11— I try to tell/share with people the gifts my horse gives to me — how she carries me in balance, her responses so sweet, soft and fluid. I have never had this experience so consistently, a horse that is so with me. She is still her own self; she tells me when she is not comfortable. It is a constant challenge for me not to over ask. She still needs training, known as language/communication skills.

Horse Training: communication teaching

2-way communication, humans teach cues – horses teach behaviorally

Humans teach horses to move on command by cue, reinforcing right response

Horses respond with behavior, body language. Horses do not think abstractly. As Mark Rashid says, they express their feelings in their actions. Their communication is almost entirely physical. Remembering that our voice is physical and can reflect unintentional, uncontrolled, emotional reaction.

Thank you for allowing these insights to flow, going into my heart to express the maturation of a childhood passion.

01/05/11 — The horse is a bridge between emotion and nature, between human and human state of mind, illusion, and the isness of nature. "Horse lives in God" I think I just read. How many times do we share the idea that time spent with our horse is better than seeing a psychiatrist? From the back of a horse we become participants in the drama of nature. The horse's awareness becomes our awareness as we tune our senses to his: a tilt of an ear, a tightening of muscle, an explosive step sideways takes us out of ourselves and into the realm of our horse. Our heart beat moves to the rhythm of the horse's hoofbeat, walking gently rocking, at the trot alert, active at the canter, our heart lifts and swells. At the gallop, our hearts sing in wild abandon.

1/10/11 — I rave about my horse to anyone who cares to listen and even to those that don't. I say I have the best horse of my life. She has balance of mind, body, and spirit. She is completely at home being a horse living in a human environment. Her body carries me without resistance, and she is a sharing conversationalist. Some of it may be about me having matured into a wiser horsewoman. But I think that wisdom merely manifests in my ability to recognize the gift in my life. My request was bequeathed. I was given the horse — a gift, not ownership, but shared time with loveliness of form, delightful interaction of mind and spirit that flows in harmony.

4/20/12 — Enthusiasm: In God, the fiery essence of God in action, contagious, inspiring, energizing. Horse and rider are becoming more than either one when enthused and inspired, each igniting the other with an electric flame passing from hand to mouth, seat to back, leg to rib, and back again. It is the bloom of shared understanding and purpose, enjoyed in the exhilaration of purpose fulfilled. I am so thankful to share a voice.

7/31/12 — Horse is the essence of Yin and Yang: active and receptive, masculine and feminine. Horse in silence is the expression of wholeness, unity, oneness. Horse knows it is one of many, learns its place in the dance of community. Community and relationship are everything, safety, procreation, health.

4/15/19 — Bridge between spirit and matter: I have repeated this so many times to help me communicate the concept and now the words evade me. With intent we guide our horse, but we never have to guide our horse home. Horse knows the way, just as our soul knows the way home, but the recalcitrant personality gets in the way, thinking it knows better. Horse, when we are skilled and in alignment, allows the use of its energy, its spirit, its body and mind. Horse gives to us completely, yet still is itself. Behaviorists talk about the social structure of dogs allowing and encouraging the initial relationship between canine and human. So it is with the horse. Horses live in family structures, social groups relying on the group dynamics for relationship, security, propagation, and education in the ways of being Horse in a predatory environment. Women often live in a predatory environment. Perhaps that is one of the similarities that draw women to horses.

Epilogue

As I sit at the computer writing, I imagine riding my horse, Sparkle Plenty. The leaves are red and gold, new green is spreading across earth dampened from autumn rain, air crisp, invigorating — a deep inhale of the exuberant breath of the season. I am not riding. I am at the computer. I haven't ridden for a year. Due to the physical changes of lives long and well lived, Sparkle Plenty and I are retired. The fluidity of body is crystallizing. She is twenty-six years old, and I am seventy-two. Even as our bodies stiffen, our spirits expand. I go out to the pasture, and she greets me with ears erect, eyes alive with expectation of goodies and grooming, head held high in anticipation. Then she canters, a bit stiff-legged, up to my heart. I love this horse; I have loved her from her birth.

I and my beloved partner, Tom, recently returned from a first-time trip to the Hawaiian Island of Kauai. I did not feel grounded until I hugged my Sparkle Plenty and rested my head on her rump, listening to the rhythmic sound of her chewing the grass hay I fed her.

My passion for horses is still there, but showing up at a new level of relationship and spirit. I peruse the old books and stories and explore new stories of the Horse/Human dynamic. I find connection in all of it and the connection is SPIRIT. Sparkle's spirit and my spirit have danced and embraced over time, place, and life changes. When I lean into her warmth, her energy, her soul, I wonder, afterwards, how I will ever live without her.

Acknowledgements

I am grateful to my writing support group, *Women Writers at The Well*. There are twelve of us that hold each other up, nurture the individual creative spirit, help to tone, shape, and inspire the unique voice we use to speak our truth. Without their embrace this book would not have happened.

Multiple thank-yous go to Dianne McCleery for telling me that this is what I was meant to write, and she was meant to midwife. She has been there every step of the way with her love of Horse.

Thank you, Joyce Campbell, for pointing out the obvious unseen by other's eyes. Thank you, Nancy Slenger, for putting some of the philosophical jargon into "other words," and reading every writing I hand you. Thank you Lorene Erickson for sharing your editing expertise, pointing out the proper placement of the parts of the book and catching last minute errors. Thank you to my life partner, Tom Sharkey, for identifying our conversation as that shared by artists. Thank you, Tom, for allowing me to see myself as an artist. Thank you to all who read the manuscript of this book and added to the polishing edits.

Thank you to Diana Rueter-Twining for giving me permission to use an image of her wonderful sculpture, *Maestro*, to illustrate our human perception of Beauty.

Thank you to my parents for seeing the passion for Horse in me when I was young and allowing me the opportunity and responsibility to own a horse in spite of their financial challenges.

A special thank you to Danae Little for her tireless help through the labyrinthian technical process of formatting and publishing this book.

Thank you to Valarie Roddy for knowing what to create for the cover of this book.

About the Author

Lynnea Paxton-Honn lives with her beloved partner, musician and song writer, Tom Sharkey, two dogs, two cats, and Sparkle Plenty, in a small Sierra Nevada foothill town known as "The Jewel of the Mother Lode."

She has a blog: heartofahorsewoman.wordpress.com that was the practice venue for this book. Her passionate love for horses is as strong as it was in the year 1951 when this story really began. She now teaches the practice of presence and oneness in meditation. Horse is the bridge that brought her to the pinnacle of Spirit.

If you have resonated with From the Heart of a Horsewoman please tell your friends and leave a review on Amazon. Thank you so much for reading and being a part of the Tribe of Horse.

www.ingramcontent.com/pod-product-compliance
Lightning Source LLC
Chambersburg PA
CBHW040803150426

42811CB00082B/2382/J